The Mad Angler

Michael Delp

THE MAD ANGLER

Mission Point Press

Copyright © 2024 by Michael Delp
All world rights reserved.

Jacket drypoint engraving and spot illustrations by Glenn Wolff.

No part of this book may be reproduced, stored in a retrieval system, or transmitted in any form or by any means electronic, mechanical, photocopying, recording or otherwise, without the prior consent of the publisher.

Readers are encouraged to go to www.MissionPointPress.com to contact the author, or to contact the publisher about how to buy this book in bulk at a discounted rate.

MISSION POINT PRESS

Published by Mission Point Press
2554 Chandler Rd.
Traverse City, MI 49696
(231) 421-9513
MissionPointPress.com

ISBN: 978-1-961302-77-8

Library of Congress Control Number: 2024911359

Printed in the United States of America

for Jack Driscoll

"One day, standing in a river with my fly rod,
I'll have the courage to admit my life."

    Jim Harrison

Contents

Introduction xi

Manifesto

The Mad Angler's Manifesto 3

The Mad Anger Finds his Spirit Animal 5

The Mad Angler Reveals His Other Spirit Animal 7

The Mad Angler's Writer's Manifesto 8

The Mad Angler Speaks the Truth to Politicians 9

The Mad Angler in the Horse Latitudes 10

The Mad Angler Ghazals 11

Lament

The Mad Angler's Lament 19

The Dream of the Mad Angler 20

The Mad Angler Contemplates Time 21

The Mad Angler as Philosopher 22

The Mad Angler Cashes It In 23

The Mad Angler Wanders Off 24

The Mad Angler's Final Lament
    (The River of a Thousand Lives) 25

Transfiguration

Transfiguration by Water
    (The Mad Angler Dissolves Away) 29

The Psalms of the Mad Angler 31

The Mad Angler in the Cathedral 34

The Mad Angler's Water Gospel 35

The Mad Angler Born Again 36

The Epiphany of the Mad Angler 37

The Mad Angler Gone AWOL 38

The Mad Angler Renders Himself 39

    Acknowledgments *41*
    About the Author *43*

Introduction

Michael Delp's Mad Angler alter ego is equal parts environmental crusader and water shaman, and his hostility toward those "feral hogs of greed" isn't so much invective or diatribe as it is an appeal for sanity in a world gone, well, mad. And at the "heart of the heart" of these poems is a voice attempting to transpose madness into song, rant into meditation, "the mist coming off the water," and in spite of the "piss swill of corporate runoff."

And so, the occasion of these persona poems is twofold: First, to confront and speak — and in direct and unavoidable proximity to those "darker hearts of developers"— the language of cherishing and its corollary, the spirit and pursuit of preservation. And secondly to foster a respect for, and to defend the ancient and abiding imperative of committed stewardship.

I say, cheers for such madness left unchecked and unapologetic, a wildness of heart that celebrates and holds every feeder creek and current, every wetland and backwater and swamp. Edgy, irate, calling out the "soul traders," the Mad Angler's passion for moving water runs deep and in the mysterious, and beautiful and oftentimes haunting images of these poems.

Jack Driscoll

The Mad Angler

Manifesto

The Mad Angler's Manifesto

I speak with the voice of water,
rivulet, brook, stream and creek,
for whitewater in lost gorges
boiling cataracts, every place
where the souls of wild fish gather
to remind us of the power of hydrology.
I speak with the name of rain,
the soft lips of condensation,
even the dew which gathers each night,
every drop another transition from sky to earth
I invoke masses of insects to take over the world,
to begin the hatching and mating, sure in the fact
that tomorrow another dam will fail, another levee crumble,
another river where you live will tire of its banks
and seek retribution on your lawn,
running up your driveway and into your basement.

I praise the flash flood,
the artesian well, the flowing hearts
under our feet,
the webs of underground rivers
coursing through solid rock.
I fish in incantations, genuflections,
my body a living marker for the crest gauge,
tidal fluctuation, flood tides and fresh water seiches.
When my eye falls on rivers, I praise their transparency,
their nature of shaping their way as they move.

Water is my heart churning in a white hydraulic,
my tongue longing for a quiet pool, the skin of night
settling in, mayflies on the edge of moonlight
sifting out of the trees.
I praise the lust for emergences,
the urge to quit the job, convert the pension funds
to river frontage,
the sudden impulse to carry a fly rod into a meeting,
the fly ripping the lips of superiors.
I embrace the chant of waterfalls,
the litany of holy rivers: Battenkill, Firehole, Bighorn.

I trust only the sweet smell of rotting cedar,
the scent of mudbanks festering with nymphs,
the rivers rising in my blood like an illness, a fever sent by
the god of desire to make his presence known, something jolting
through the veins to replace the done deal, the raise
with a corner office, the soul trader
you most likely have become.

The Mad Angler Finds His Spirit Animal

For weeks he baits crows into the yard, uses
road kill opossums, porcupines, the skulls of deer.

When the river sky is dark with crows,
he slips into his suit of dark feathers,
dances out into the yard,
grabs the largest crow and
takes him inside.

In the tool shed, he makes a cut in his chest,
slips the crow under his skin,
then walks up three flights of stairs
to the attic, then the roof,
where he makes that wild plunge to the ground below.

When he comes to, he sees that he has the vision
of a crow, that the night is now endless,
and he has the capacity to fly out of his life,
his only mark of passing, a few lost feathers
left like trail markers,
and for decades after he leaves
you will hear his
voice each time a crow passes over,
that familiar caw, caw, caw
transformed on his blue crow tongue
into rivers, rivers, rivers.

The Mad Angler Reveals
His Other Spirit Animal

Thirty years ago a wolverine crawled into my heart
and has stayed all these years.
He eats snow and chunks of ice or the bitter flesh of failure
I pass down to him like so much bread.
It's almost as if he is living under the front porch.
He watches everything and at night
I hear him cough up his dreams.
He wants to go out in the yard,
but will attack everything that moves,
so I keep him lodged in close, no leash, no rope, not even a collar.
He loves it inside me, claims there is a certain mist in my heart
which he prefers to sunlight.
I would have given him a name long ago,
but he says he doesn't need one.
He sniffs the air and tells me what's coming to dismantle me.
He circles like a dog before he sleeps,
but when I reach in to pet him, there's nothing there
but coarse hair wrapped around a muscle beating itself to death.

The Mad Anglers Writer's Manifesto

Think of every poem as water.
Think of that water dammed, channeled, culverted,
bottled, ditched, diverted, and generally throttled.
Or: the elderly woman stuck in a kitchen band with
saxophones lodged in her bones,
or lap dogs parked on the porch
who yearn to wander the neighbor's garbage cans
suddenly turned into Great Pyrenees Mountain dogs
off the leash for good,
or that vision you once had of yourself as a writer
drawn through the needle's eye of too much school,
the lectures by the boring
for the bored to keep them still and thinking that poetry
is something to cut up like a pig in a biology class,
when what you have left is only the parts
and nothing of the pigness.
Think of the sky filled with stones instead of wandering clouds,
or the wings of birds made of concrete
instead of mostly the air in their bones, or think
of the skin of the person you love wrapped in lovely barbed wire,
of the sun sitting in the sky as a bowling ball giving off darkness.
Then, think of that water up there
in the beginning of this manifesto suddenly turned
loose, winding, meandering, pausing in a slow eddy,
then coursing, falling, into
the sweet madness of poetry itself.

The Mad Angler Speaks Truth to Politicians

Over seventy years ago, as soon as I could walk,
I abandoned myself to water.
I prowled lakes and creeks, rivers and swamps.
Now, I sit on the edge of the woods
where river meets sky and I tell you this:
As surely as water is blood,
as surely as my blood is water,
what you have done over decades of greed
has turned your hearts into pus pumps.
I would trade most of you for a single river.
You have done enough and your
malignant work is done.
Had I the power, I would banish you
to a nation made entirely of sand,
a black sun in a black sky, no rain,
each one of you exiled to a tiny hut
beside a river made of oil where not even
your sandy tears would make a difference.

The Mad Angler in the Horse Latitudes

Though thousands of miles away,
the Mad Angler can feel the Horse Latitude air
hanging in grey sheets over the river,
dry and subsiding,
no fish rising and his heart stalled again
trying to leave his body to rendezvous
with another heart, deeper under ground.
He rises, walks out to the deck
announces his arrival in the kingdom of fish, but no one cares.
His voice flies only so far,
then catches like a husk in a dead Ash,
resting there until September when it falls away,
washes downriver as if it were a perfect poem
never written, never seen.

The Mad Angler Ghazals

    I.

He watches the darkness walk up out of the river and slide
    under his skin.
In his veins, he mistakes it for wine.

He walks the river at night, running his hands
    underwater.
This is sleep he says, his tongue's cartography old and worn.

Sometimes you see him, up in the trees, his arms like wings.
He is the crow flying at night. The dark bird entering your
    thighs.

Some nights the mad angler dances the moon out of the sky,
    the sun, the stars.
All summer he lets his body wander by itself in the dark bed
    of the river.

Over a small fire he burns his tongue, sifts his ashes,
Calls himself a fire poet, smoke poet, leaves his bones
    dreaming in the embers.

2.

Oh mad one, the moons you seek are no longer in the sky.
Look inside your heart where they are shrinking as you read.

I gave my heart away for ten buckets of river water.
Tonight I dream them running down my naked back.

Another kind of moon lost somewhere inside her thighs.
My fingers seek her wondrous heat, the real moon just rising.

Twenty years ago I mortgaged my tongue, nailed it to the
      door.
Tonight, the mad angler comes home, rips it down and
      breathes again.
What you give away he says, you can take back.
I give this, I want to say, offering my life, taken back again and
      again.

3.

The wind comes up, runs down the spine of the river.
The mad angler is on the bank, cutting down the small fruits of
    darkness.

Up on the ridges coyotes lick the backs of shadows.
The mad one feels his guard hairs bristle, a new country in
    his head.

He builds an altar: the dry bones of winter-killed deer,
then lights a fire, his hands slide in first, become the white
    embers of one river god.

I have seen him always by himself, the mad angler alive, but not
    alive,
Walking upriver, the river cleaving, each stone on the bottom a
    bright coal.
When he sleeps, the river vanishes, moons rise in his heart,
    coyotes everywhere.

4.

There are no days in the week. No months.
Only the slow seepage of the mad one's ideas.

In the dark ribbon of sleep, he moves through
        swamps,
thoughts falling from his skin like invisible trail markers.

He knows those who follow are already lost.
He loses himself. Turns in all directions. Drives his mind into
        the ground like a stake.

He knows exactly where he is, and finds himself looking up
into a sky filled with black clouds, his dry skin praying for the
        poetry of rain.

    5.

He sends his books down the river,
one by one they slip away, each word turning wild.

For weeks he denies the power of words, instead:
Talks the talk of bark, willow, the hard tongue of ironwood.

Six crows scrape the yard, pick up the mad angler's shadow.
For an instant there is a dark flag in the sky, then only dust.

He knows the correct angle of the dance in his legs
when he will suddenly turn from man to crow to the prophet
    of rivers.

What he says is unspeakable. He wants no followers. No
    Bible.
Only the haunted memory of the one tree where he has nailed
    his rabid skin.

Lament

The Mad Angler's Lament

for Jim Harrison

Either everything counts or nothing does,
no middle ground these days,
yet I navigate the dark
tangled river between these two countries of counting and not counting,
never knowing on which side to set up camp, build a fire,
find enough coals to continue on, praying for some direction
to rise up out of the ash.

Tonight, in a clear dark sky,
the entire constellation of Sagittarius flared,
then vanished, and I was sure
I heard the sound of the giant hooves
of God's horse, either approaching
or riding away,
wondered what the difference was between them,
wanting more than ever for it to be
on His way toward me,
readying myself,
prepared to be scooped up and carried off in those warm saddlebags,
Jim's voice steadying the ride.

The Dream of the Mad Angler

for Claudia and Jaime

My flesh was water,
and when I stepped into the river
I disappeared.
I drank moonlight in the dark
and whispered my name like a prayer.
When I stepped back into my house,
no one knew who I was.
I thought I recognized myself
in the rooms I'd haunted,
but when I fell into my own bed,
beside my wife,
I felt my skin stretching out,
trailing off for miles through the woods,
felt myself turning back into this dream river
where I wait each night for my daughter,
the exquisite arc of her casting,
the absolute hymn of the line
slipping through her fingers,
and my wife, standing on the bank
calling what used to be my name.

The Mad Angler Contemplates Time

Coursing toward old age, he steps into the river,
throws his watch into the current and spends an evening
counting time with the rhythm of a bouncing cedar sweeper
caught in the wash along the bank.
He speaks in time declensions:
time burning down, burning daylight,
his life a candle,
a wick made of flesh.
He howls into the night air at the notion of The Rapture,
knowing full well that on the last day, at the last minute,
all rivers will suddenly angle up toward the sky,
then drop like a spear through his heart.

The Mad Angler as Philosopher

Life is mostly muzzle flash, sunlight on water,
nothing more,
your body a creek without a name.
Dance for all you're worth in the middle of any river.
Sleep is an aquifer, the mind a well.
Think of the surface of a river
as something to be hammered
with endless casts.
Chase silence, the wisdom of cedar sweepers.
Trade your lips for fins.
Think of immortality as just another way
to step into the same river more than once.

The Mad Angler Cashes It In

The mortgage burned, ashes in the tomato garden,
nothing left in the yard save an abandoned Jeep,
and he's off, out the door, one rod in his hand,
the river rising miles from him, but somehow,
directly in front of him,
something he regards as a daily miracle.
What the river gives him is like food, like air, and there are times
when he strips down, simply attaches himself to a submerged log
and lets his body drift in the current,
the sun like a bright disk above him, or at night, the
moon, a milky eye, or that ancient face,
man in the moon mouth telling him
there is no other way to live.

Suspended in current, he empties himself, is emptied of what
sluices out of the mind, yet something stays,
becomes particulate in his blood,
turns into a language that only others who love rivers will recognize.

These others are like a clan, like a flock of birds always moving in
a murmuration of flesh, and head, and water, their
lives joined by logjams, back eddies,
wet clay and the way their hearts have shaped themselves
to whatever comes to wash them away.

The Mad Angler Wanders Off

The rods, gone,
reels and empty whiskey bottles melted down to silver puddles,
the ash of bamboo
mixed with the ash of ancient cedar kindling,
the words repeated over the flames and smoke
meant only to offer up a prayer
for no one else to hear,
how to leave for a better place,
a spot to watch the stars wheeling
from a high ridge above the creek,
a place further in, unmappable
the mind counting steps only to know how far to get beyond,
to forget the way back.

The hut entrance is long and narrow,
enters the hillside and goes down,
steps made of roots and glacial till.
The entry made to collapse,
the songs carried by a flute made of bone,
no singing but the hum of the world
marking time,
the days left to conjure,
then scrawl a poem once a year on birch bark,
blood words, water words, root words,
the plan, to scatter the floor with them,
read them back to his dancing shadow, barely visible in the dim,
pine pitch light.

The Mad Angler's Final Lament
(The River of a Thousand Lives)

for Chris Dombrowski

Brutal and stumbling, back-watered,
through the swamp of the heart
into this place where rivers are born,
the sky full of rising cumulus and wind,
every sacred tree singing the water into existence,
up from ancient aquifers,
brought by centuries of rain,
my mind catches itself in a still pool reflection,
the squint to see more deeply,
followed by the failure of language to describe the journey in,
the way down, thoughts dying off, passing into darkness,
the pulse of wings against the chest,
body a vessel rocking in the night current, swaying itself to sleep,
the rising and falling of feeling so many lives passing through me,
moon coming up, another reflection to stare into,
moon-eyed and transfixed
watching the soul walk away from the skin,
into the river, die another time, and another, and another,
come back weeping, my mouth open to the constant flow,
the churning tongues of water entering my bloodstream,
clots of words deposited all along the course of the inner river,
a self on the banks lifting those sacred messages
into the bloody cistern where poems come back to life.

Transfiguration

Transfiguration by Water
(The Mad Angler Dissolves Away)

I remember only this: my spine dissolved
and disappeared in the river.
When I crawled from the bank in the morning,
I spit words onto the table, watched them
drop off the edge and into a blue bowl,
then charted them all day trying to arrange themselves
into a language I might know.
I set the bowl on the ground and watched the words mix
with the images of passing
clouds. Nothing came. For weeks.
I sat through cold, frost, and then one night, under a half-moon,
almost below freezing, I felt my legs go in separate directions,
my lungs, floating in mid-air,
called in a pack of coyotes.
What came next I can not completely tell, but there was loping,
howling, my nose soaked in blood.
Now, that deep snarl I hear in town when I walk past strangers
will not go away.
I ache for the moon, the scent of bloody fur,
and that final memory of the last night I
entered the river to cleanse myself of
everything human I could remember.

The Psalms of the Mad Angler

I

This daily summer ritual:
walking up towards the ridge in the middle
of a feeder creek,
stopping at the pool just below the rock ledge,
dipping, first my hands and then my head,
my ears burning with the sound of roiled water.
My scalp numbs, then my eyes,
and if only for an instant, I retrieve my savage name:
"HE- WHO-SEES-AS-A-RIVER."
Working my way back to the cabin,
half-blind,
I feel my way through the trees.
My feet know the way through deadfall,
and those wild crows overhead...
they chant the way to the door.

2

I wanted to write the sky full of black poems, but the moon refused,
so I wrote the voice of water.
I spoke the seams of current,
thought of them as you would the seams in a silk blouse,
how lovely the breasts float under a skein of white.
Then, I spoke the rest of the dream up into her body,
and when she stepped towards me,
I felt the spray of her moving hips,
the very watery-ness of her voice as it tongued its way
through the wild hair on my skin.

3

I drink water. I make water. I am a cloud in the flesh,
a river eddied in my heart,
I speak words and wish they were rain,
and every day I wake to trade the liquid behind my eyes
for a chance to see past the surfaces of lakes.

4

There is humidity in my blood,
storms forming in my cells.
Each week is an accumulation and a loss,
so much time like so much water over a dam,
standing next to deep current thinking
that I could hold a cupped hand of water to my
ear and someday, if I had my mind right,
it would tell me what it knows.

The Mad Angler in the Cathedral

He spends a year removing the vaulted roof
fueled by the desire
to look up at night into a sanctuary of stars.
When he works, he speaks the names of ghosts, the liturgy of
entomology embedded in the dark water of his brain...
He believes in the gospel of intricate casts,
the psalms of mending line,
and drinking from the baptismal font, he prays
that all the angels might drift down, the sound of hymns
replaced by the singing of the fly lines they cast over the heads
of bait fishermen.
In the end, he tears down the walls,
channels a river through the pews,
and waits in the rain for the wild god of trout
to turn each swimming miracle loose from his hands.

The Mad Angler's Water Gospel

Meditate on this: your own skin cleansed for days in the river
as one might wash a bed sheet, then
hung to dry in the sun, left overnight to soak up the mist
coming off the water, dried again in the sun and decorated
with fish paintings rendered in your blood.
Imagine it now, furling and unfurling in a July breeze,
riding the air like a prayer flag.
Stepping close, pressing it to your face
you would smell again the deep, abiding scent of cedar,
better than any perfume.

Meditate on this also: to ever wear this skin again
is to say that water
is in the bucket that fuels the soul,
that it might seek lower ground,
those safe places to gather itself
before it vanishes into the sky.

The Mad Angler Born Again

It comes in summer, maybe late June, a night in full moonlight,
he never knows, but knows the marrow pull of moon path,
the constant thrum in his blood
that he has an emptiness which needs to be filled.
He comes to the river to make amends, seeking atonement
for the sins of fishing with bait as a child,
the souls of countless bluegills
haunting the buried structure of his dreams.
He comes to get right with the gods of water,
those invisible ones always whispering in his ears about bad casts,
weak knots, their oft-ignored warnings
about hungry maidens in dark waters.
Where this happens is as much a cathedral as Notre Dame,
cedars vaulted into the sky over a congregation of insects.

This madman stands in full current, bends low,
spreads his hands out, reading the scripture of water,
the living psalm of the river.
Something in his head breaks loose, swirls,
comes up out of the dimly lit darkness
and sees the world as it was meant to be:
water, moonlight, mile after mile of the river's blood
flowing through him,
all those maidens shedding their lovely, translucent skins.

The Epiphany of the Mad Angler

When they called for my intellect, I told them
it was dead,
buried at the end of some worthless two-track
with a box of textbooks,
then I walked to the river to live among the fish,
and when they asked for my instincts
I told them I made a trade for the sense
that rides on the surface of the river.
I knew that sense instantly when I learned
that the water of rivers
collects and eddies, not in pools,
but in dark pockets of wisdom,
places under sweeping cedars
where river stones have arranged themselves
into messages,
a kind of Braille,
places where the tongue of a man
wants to slide out of his head,
swim away.

The Mad Angler Gone AWOL

Hard to imagine him more feral,
wandering thickets in search of brook trout, miles from his truck,
bent down and crawling through swamp muck,
his possessions long ago sold off,
his name expunged from public records,
his birth certificate altered to his alias, "Mad Dog," no last name.
He spends his nights at small campfires
eating what he catches or steals from gardens,
his life imagined as a tapestry of heroic adventures,
dangerous attempts every night ingesting hot coals
to find their meaning,
drinking deeply from stagnant water
to replenish his tattered imagination,
his arms and legs rubbed raw
from thrashing through miles of lost territory,
those places inside him where he dwells on his errors,
the map inside him curling toward its center,
the compass spinning in his wild head.

The Mad Angler Renders Himself

"Rendering: a term for melting and clarifying"

This heart, part Wolverine, part bird of prey,
will never stop beating even into the next life,
and once freed from the body,
will fly through darkness using its own light,
no longer muscle but made of all those poems
taken in and wrapped,
like tissue around a pure ember of spirit, decades of memory,
dead poets whispering from an outer darkness,
their words flaming,
as if this comet inside my chest
were able to take in the fuel of each syllable,
this voyage part blood,
part bone, and that white, ghosting tail
alive, shooting star, glowing dust.

Acknowledgments

Some of these poems have appeared in *The Dunes Review*, and in two collections of poetry: "Lying in the River's Dark Bed" and "The Last Good Water," from Wayne State University Press. Special thanks to Chad Pastotnik at Deep Wood Press for the publication of the handmade *Mad Angler Chapbook*, printed in a limited edition of 71 copies. In addition, the Mad Angler poems are the inspiration for the Mad Angler Estate Series of Mad Angler Whiskey, Mad Angler Bourbon and Mad Angler Rye from the Ironfish Distillery in Thompsonville, Michigan.

My gratitude to Glenn Wolff for his cover, back cover and interior illustrations, and to Troy Anderson of Ironfish Distillery for his photographic work as the basis for the front cover.

Special thanks to Jaime Delp, Jim Olson and Grant Parsons for their editing suggestions.

About the Author

Michael Delp lives and fishes in Northern Michigan. He is the author of several collections of poetry and a collection of short stories from Wayne State University Press. He is the former Director of Creative Writing at Interlochen Arts Academy and is also Co-editor Emeritus of the award-winning "Made in Michigan" book series from Wayne State University Press.

Milton Keynes UK
Ingram Content Group UK Ltd.
UKHW010832040724
444921UK00011BA/136/J

9 781961 302778